Chiara Lubich

Servant of Unity

by
Jim Gallagher

*All booklets are published thanks to the
generous support of the members of the
Catholic Truth Society*

CATHOLIC TRUTH SOCIETY
PUBLISHERS TO THE HOLY SEE

Contents

All rights reserved. First published 2015 by The Incorporated Catholic Truth Society, 40-46 Harleyford Road London SE11 5AY Tel: 020 7640 0042 Fax: 020 7640 0046. Copyright © 2015 The Incorporated Catholic Truth Society.

ISBN 978 1 78469 078 6

A Precious Spiritual Legacy

When the local bishop officially opened the Cause of Chiara Lubich in January 2015 his cathedral in Frascati, the beautiful hill town outside Rome, was full to overflowing. The ceremony was watched worldwide at over eighteen thousand viewing points. Moreover, it wasn't only Catholics who were present in that sixteenth century cathedral but members of other Christian denominations and even other religions.

As if to prove, if proof were needed, that this was no "ordinary" beginning of a Cause, the Pope himself sent a message, signed by his Secretary of State, and read out by a former Secretary of State, to the assembled devotees of this Italian woman who had died only seven years previously. Encouraging those engaged in the Cause who "conserve the precious spiritual legacy" of the foundress of the Work of Mary, he exhorted them to "make known to the People of God the life and work of one who welcomed Our Lord's invitation and ignited a new light for the Church on the journey towards unity".

That this journey towards unity in the Lord was not limited to the confines of the Catholic Church was evident at the funeral of this small, humble woman who hailed from the north of Italy.

A funeral like no other

On that day in March 2008, before the Requiem Mass began in the Roman basilica of St Paul's-Outside-the-Walls, members of other Christian denominations and other religions (and people of no religious faith) were given an opportunity to say a word. A Buddhist monk in his striking saffron robes knelt down on the floor to venerate the simple coffin containing the mortal remains of Chiara, then he stood up to give his message. "Dear friends, you Christians, you Catholics, you must remember: Chiara belongs not only to you. She belongs to all of us!"

It was a simple but striking reminder of how this most loyal and devoted daughter of the Church had reached out to all people of goodwill and had been welcomed to give her Christian witness to gatherings of Buddhists, to Sikhs, and even to a black community mosque in Harlem.

Her simple and dignified funeral was itself illustration of a phrase once given to Chiara as a gift. After Chiara had given her Christian witness to several thousand adherents of a lay Buddhist movement in Japan, its founder presented her with a typical oriental fan. Among the beautiful illustrations decorating it, in the finest calligraphy was the phrase "He who gives his life completely to God will see thousands of other souls come to life all around him."

Chiara gives her Christian testimony at the Malcolm X mosque in Harlem, New York.

Church and State, Town and Gown Represented

And at that funeral Mass, celebrated by four cardinals, forty bishops and several hundred priests, thousands of people clamoured to pay tribute to this unassuming woman who had inspired them to follow God ever more closely. With the basilica full to capacity, the crowds gathered outside could follow the ceremony on giant video screens normally used at large papal events. Around the world, many thousands of gatherings were held to follow events on the live internet link-up and satellite broadcasts.

Civil society was present with representatives carrying the banners of communities the length and breadth of Italy who had previously made Chiara an "honorary citizen" of their town or village. Academia was there, too, with representatives of many of those universities around the world which had awarded her honorary doctorates for her enlightening work in the field of theology, spirituality, economy, sociology and social communication.

Yet, throughout her life, Chiara Lubich had never sought the approval of men. For her to do the Will of God was all-in-all. Her assurance that she was doing just that lay in the approval of her local bishop, and above all in unity with the Holy Father, Christ's Vicar on Earth.

Benedict XVI: "This Our Sister"

The reigning pontiff at the time, Pope Benedict XVI, sent his Secretary of State to celebrate Chiara's funeral Mass. The cardinal also read out a personal message sent by the Pope himself.

> So many are the reasons for giving thanks to God for the gift given to the Church in this woman of dauntless faith, a gentle messenger of hope and of peace, the foundress of a vast spiritual family which encompasses multiple fields of evangelisation.
>
> I would like above all to thank Him for the service that Chiara rendered to the Church: a silent and insightful service, always in harmony with the Magisterium of the Church. "The popes" she said, "have always understood us." And this because Chiara and the Work of Mary have sought to respond with docile fidelity to every one of their appeals and wishes. The uninterrupted link with my venerable predecessors, from the Servant of God Pius XII to Blessed John XXIII, to the Servants of God Paul VI, John Paul I and John Paul II is concrete testimony to that. The sure guiding light for her was the thinking of the Pope. So, looking at the initiatives which she generated, one might even affirm that she somehow had the prophetic ability to intuit it and enact it in advance… May the God of hope welcome the soul of this our sister.

That the visible head of the Church on earth could appreciate her work and publicly pray for "this our sister" would be grace indeed for this humble daughter of the Church. Once, in conversation with her housemates, she was asked what she would like on her tombstone. She replied that all she would want would be an image of the dome of St Peter's.

Every day, she and all her thousands of spiritual brothers and sisters, sons and daughters, consecrated to God in the Work that she founded, prayed: "Jesus, who lives in the Most Holy Eucharist, we - individually and all together - promise you above all to be among ourselves the realization of your New Commandment: to love one another as you have loved us, even to being abandoned by the Father....Make (of us) one single soul, and may you consecrate this soul to the Blessed Virgin, your Mother, so that in some manner she maybe spiritually present in it."

Childhood

Silvia Lubich, the second of four children, was born on 22nd January 1920 in the city of Trent in northern Italy. That city had until two years previously been part of the Austro-Hungarian empire and was, of course, famous for the sixteenth century Church Council held there.

Her parents Luigi and Luigia had married on the Feast of the Assumption of Our Lady, 15th August 1916. They had met in the newspaper printworks where they both worked after Luigi returned injured from the First World War. The mother, Luigia, was a daily Mass-goer, and quite openly kept her Missal on top of her work station. Luigi, on the other hand, was not then a practising Catholic and was classed as a socialist, and would even at one stage be branded a communist.

The rise of Benito Mussolini and the Fascist Party that he founded the year before Silvia/Chiara's birth would have profound implications for the young Lubich family.

Silvia was baptised in Trent's church of St Mary Major the day after her birth. (In later life her name was changed to Chiara.) As she grew, her mother remembered her being an obedient child, who enjoyed playing with her older brother Gino, and helping to look after her two younger sisters. She always did her school homework well and was a neat and tidy child.

Prays to Jesus in the Eucharist

Chiara remembered that from the age of six, probably as she began being prepared for her First Holy Communion, she began praying intensely before the Eucharist. Gazing at the tabernacle or at the Blessed Sacrament exposed on the altar, she would pray, "Lord, you who are light and warmth, enter me through my eyes." For the rest of her life she would nurture a burning devotion to Jesus present in the Eucharist and she would do much of her studying and her writing on her knees before the tabernacle.

In October 1922 the King of Italy asked Mussolini to form a government. After elections in 1924 when the Fascists won three-quarters of the parliamentary seats, the following year saw the passing of the *Fascistissime Laws* which would create a real Fascist dictatorship. Catholic organisations such as the Scouts were banned. Membership in the *Italian Youth* became obligatory, though much of the time Chiara and Gino conveniently "forgot" to attend their gatherings held on Saturday mornings.

Fascist Laws

A political police force, OVRA (the *Organisation for Vigilance and Repression of Anti-Fascist Activity*) was formed. The newspaper where Luigi worked, *Il Popolo*, was suppressed. Chiara's father Luigi refused to carry the Fascist party card, even though it would surely help him get work somewhere. Undaunted, he and a friend set up as traders in fine wines. Business was good at first and the family lived comfortably. Chiara later remembered that they could even enjoy summer holidays in the Dolomite mountains. One of her earliest memories was of the sense of space and freedom there in the Dolomites - and also speeding down the hillside on a home-made sled with her brother Gino.

Alas, the idyllic childhood life was not to last. In 1929 there was the Wall Street Crash. The effects of the Great Depression soon spread across the Atlantic, and in 1930 Luigi's business collapsed. Although he was the father of a young family, he stuck by his principles. He would not sign up to Fascism, even though others begged him at least to call on his former "association" with Il Duce. This referred to an incident in his younger days, before his marriage. While he was working on the production side of *Il Popolo* during the night, he rented a room in Trent where he slept during the day. His landlord asked him if he wouldn't mind if he rented out that same room in the night-time to someone who worked dayshifts. That someone was Benito Mussolini, who was then an assistant editor on the newspaper of Cesare Battisti. Until 1918 Trent was an Austrian city. Battisti, Mussolini and so many others were "patriots" who called for a united Italy. Battisti was hanged by the Austrians in 1916.

Now, in the 1930s, people would urge Luigi Lubich to contact Il Duce to remind him of a great favour he had done him: when the Austrians were coming to arrest Mussolini, Luigi was able to warn him, and Benito escaped.

First Illness: bearing it through Love

At the age of ten also Chiara had her first personal experience of illness. She fell seriously ill with appendicitis and resulting peritonitis. The doctor who operated on her said that only about one person in a thousand survived it at that time. However, as Chiara later remembered, "I came through and recovered completely, thanks to the prayers of the Sisters and my parents. I think that it was from that time that I began to know the presence of suffering in my life, and the possibility of bearing it through love."

As the Great Depression continued, life became more and more difficult for the Lubich family. While the parents often went without in order to feed their family, the children never went hungry. Friends and neighbours remember that Luigia, the mother, was a skilled seamstress and made all the children's clothes. So while the family knew extremely straitened circumstances, and had very, very little, they never actually looked destitute.

The young Chiara in fact became the main breadwinner while still a school pupil. From the age of thirteen, as well as doing her own school work and studies, she began to tutor other children. She would tutor them in Italian, maths and particularly in geography.

Disagrees with Teacher

At the age of fifteen, in 1935, Chiara felt a call to give her life for Christ, to be a martyr. She said "yes" unreservedly. She did well in all subjects at school. In the philosophy class in high school she contradicted and argued with the teacher, who was an atheist. Chiara later remembered that he "used to speak in an inexact manner" about Our Lady and the Catholic Church. "This hurt and annoyed me," she said in later life, "especially because I was afraid that my classmates would accept what he was saying."

Despite her combats with him, at the end of the year he gave her the top mark. Some years later he wrote to her and told her, "I've begun praying to that God you believe in."

As the end of her time at the *Istituto Antonio Rosmini* teacher-training school in Trent approached, Chiara longed to continue her studies. She felt sure that the search for truth and beauty would be paramount at the one Catholic university then accessible to lay people. In 1921, the Franciscan priest Agostino Gemelli, convert from agnosticism and member of a leading Masonic family, had founded the Catholic University of the Sacred Heart in Milan. Gemelli was a doctor but in those days the Church forbade priests to practise medicine (the Gemelli Polyclinic in Rome is now part of the medical faculty of the Sacred Heart University).

"I will be your teacher"

Anyway, with great hope Chiara filled out all the application forms to be accepted to study at the University of the Sacred Heart. There were only twenty free places available. Of the hundreds of applicants, Chiara came twenty-third. In her family's straitened circumstances, there was no way she could afford to pay for university. She was devastated. She broke down and wept. As she cried on her mother's shoulder, she suddenly perceived a clear and strong interior voice telling her, "Fear not. I myself will be your teacher".

Chiara was eventually accepted to study philosophy at the University of Venice. Attendance was obligatory only a few days per term, most study being done at home. When the war broke out and roads became impassable, even those few days' attendance stopped and everything came to a halt.

Meanwhile, still in 1939, Chiara would travel the furthest that she had so far been from home. She was a member of the Catholic lay apostolate, *Catholic Action*, in the student division. Her local student branch decided to sponsor her to attend the national *Catholic Action* student congress to be held that year in Loreto, about three hundred and fifty kilometres from Trent.

Not far from Ancona in the Marche region of Italy, Loreto had been famous since at least the thirteenth century as the site of the Holy House. This was believed to have been the home of the Holy Family of Jesus, Mary and Joseph in Nazareth. There were various stories, legends and beliefs as to how this came to be transported to Italy. It is today inside a large church built around it and accorded the dignity of a basilica. (Pope Benedict XVI visited it in 2012, to mark the fiftieth anniversary of a visit by Pope St John XXIII.)

Holy House of Loreto

Chiara was never one given to displays of emotion (which made her "admission" of weeping when being refused entry to Milan university so difficult). But upon entering the "little house" of Loreto for the first time, she was swathed in tears.

She wasn't thinking about her future "way" in life or any sort of vocation. She was, she remembered later, just another young woman, living life to the full, enjoying her studies, part of a humble but happy family. Yet inside that little house, she recalled,

> I found myself plunged, immersed in this great mystery. I began to meditate on all that might have happened within those walls: the family life of Jesus, Mary and Joseph. I touched with great veneration the stones and

the beams. I seemed to hear the voice of the child Jesus. I imagined him crossing the room. I was looking at those walls which had had the good fortune to hear the voice and the songs of Mary.

While Chiara dutifully attended all the talks, lectures and discussions held in the congress venue in Loreto, she later recalled that whenever the other girls would retire for rest or relaxation time to the school where they were being put up, she would run to the shrine, in order to get right inside the "little house".

And each time it had the same effect on her, causing the same deep emotion. "It was as if a particular grace of God was enveloping me completely, almost as if the Divine Will was overwhelming me," she recounted to her biographer half a century later. "It was all contemplation, prayer, as if in some way I was living with the three persons of the Holy Family."

This experience, this perception and awareness of the "home life" of the Holy Family would mark her and be a feature of all that she did for the rest of her life.

At the end of the congress there was a High Mass in the basilica which sheltered the Holy House. What Chiara experienced during that liturgy in Loreto was the culmination and crowning point of the mysterious and mystical hours she had spent in the "little house".

The church was full to bursting point with all these Catholic students. There were some boys there but the majority were girls - all wearing their white mantillas. Somehow during that High Mass, while everyone was attentively following proceedings in their missals, I knew that I had found my "way". It was a "fourth way". Then I had an image of a whole host of white-clad virgins following me on this way. I didn't know what it meant, but that's what I experienced.

Chiara had graduated from the teacher-training facility in 1938 with top marks. The first year as a teacher, she did supply work in a couple of little villages in the region. She got the pupils involved in *Catholic Action* and also attended Holy Mass every day. The predominantly elderly matrons who frequented that daily Mass were impressed by the demeanour of their young schoolmistress. She was always so well turned out! She had a dignity of bearing and style that others noticed.

When she returned from her 1939 trip to Loreto, her pupils and also her parish priest were keen to know how it went. To the priest, who knew her well, all she could say was, "I've found my way." However, to describe it all she could do was say what it was not; it wasn't marriage, it wasn't religious life in a convent, it wasn't being as a single person dedicated hermit-like to God while living in the world. It was her "fourth way".

Favourite Teacher

Life continued as normal for the next few years, at least as normal as wartime circumstances allowed. In 1940 she obtained a post as a teacher at the Seraphic College, a school for orphans run by the local Capuchin Franciscans. She was a gifted and empathetic teacher. In later life some of the boys recalled how they used to long for "play-time" to end so that they could get back into class with Miss Lubich.

Also, there were no ready-made "resources" such as we find today. Chiara herself drew up posters with exquisitely hand-drawn pictures to illustrate numbers and the letters of the alphabet.

The fathers of the Capuchin community could tell that they were dealing with not only a gifted young teacher, but a young woman of great spiritual depth and wisdom. Sometime in 1943 they invited her to become a member of the Franciscan Third Order, an association of laypeople who followed the Franciscan spirituality and met regularly for spiritual exercises led by the Capuchins. As Chiara later explained, apart from the lay apostolate, encouraged by the Pope, of *Catholic Action*, this was the only type of spiritual involvement available for young laywomen in her area.

Taking a new name

As was customary at that time, upon being received into
the Third Order she took a new name, a "name in religion".
She chose Chiara, the Italian for Clare. Asked in later life
why, she explained that she read a biography of St Clare
of Assisi which told how the twelfth century saint, when
asked by St Francis what she desired, replied "God". In
the Bull of Canonisation it seemed to be all "light, charity;
charity, light", explained Chiara. From then on Silvia
Lubich was known as Chiara, even by her family.

Shortly after this her mother Luigia asked Chiara to run
an errand one morning. She was to go to a nearby hamlet
(called Madonna Bianca) to fetch some fresh milk. On
her way there, under a railway viaduct passing overhead,
Chiara suddenly became aware of a strong steady voice
within. "Give yourself completely to me," it said.

"I'll never be alone"

Chiara dropped a note immediately to her priest confessor
asking permission to take a private vow of total consecration
in chastity to Almighty God. When the priest discussed this
with her in order to discern the veracity of her vocation, he
asked whether she realised that by renouncing marriage
and a family, and not entering a traditional religious
community, she would one day find herself alone, all alone
in the world, maybe ending up in an old people's home?
Chiara's reply was, "As long as there is a tabernacle on

earth, as long as the Eucharistic presence is in the world, I shall never be alone."

With this and the rest of their discussions, the priest was convinced, and granted her permission to make her private vow. Thus, on 7th December 1943, the vigil of the Feast of the Immaculate Conception, she rose in the cold dark of the early morning, put on her finest frock and made her way through a storm to the chapel for a 6 a.m. Mass.

She remembered how battling through the raging storm in the dark of the early hours seemed to be a sign of how she must struggle to attain God, of how a hostile power would fight against her way to God. Then, as she approached the friary in whose chapel the Mass would be offered, the scene changed; the huge gates opened up before her as she approached. She laughed in later life as she recounted how no doubt a gate-keeper saw her approach and opened the gates, but as a young woman struggling through the storm to reach her destination, it felt like a spiritual sign that God himself was preparing the way for her.

I married God

In the stillness of that small chapel, while the wind howled outside, there was only Chiara present and then entered the priest who would celebrate the Holy Mass. During that Mass the twenty-three-year-old Chiara gave herself in perpetual chastity to the exclusive service of God himself. "It was as if I had married God," she later remembered.

Just before Holy Communion she had a completely clear interior vision. It was as if she were walking across a bridge. As she moved forward, the bridge behind her crumbled and she realised that what she was doing was not just reciting a formula. Before the consecrated host held aloft she would pronounce the words "I make the vow of perfect and perpetual chastity". In fact she was leaving behind her whole life as she knew it; her family, her friends, her recreations and all that was familiar to her.

Previously the priest had also told Chiara that as it was such a privileged moment, she should not be afraid to ask God for any very special request. She wrote down her "special request" on a little piece of paper which the priest placed under the chalice during Mass.

Chiara had told no one of her special early-morning appointment. After the Mass and her moments of thanksgiving, she left the chapel to rush home, stopping on the way to buy three red carnations to place before the crucifix in her bedroom.

Before leaving the house after five o'clock that morning, she had tried to keep a vigil with the Lord, as suggested by the priest. In the cold December night as she knelt before her crucifix, she noticed that the corpus, the figure of Our Lord on the cross, had misted over with the heat from her breath. This seemed to say to her that her way ahead, her spirituality, would not be so much focused on the dreadful physical sufferings of the Lord's Passion and crucifixion, but on his spiritual interior suffering. And so it would prove to be.

From the moment of that total self-donation, that commitment - of which she had told no one - others seemed to notice a change in her and be drawn to her. Even the priests of the Capuchin friary noticed that other young women and girls seemed to seek her out and want to be in her company. One of the priests asked Chiara if she would give a little talk one Sunday afternoon in the parish hall.

Finding Companions

A young local woman, then nineteen years old, had briefly flirted with the idea of becoming a nun but didn't. She had lost her father two years previously and was now, in 1943, working as a secretary at the Trent Chamber of Commerce. Her confessor, one of the Capuchin priests, invited her to attend a sort of day retreat on a Sunday. Natalia Dallapiccola later remembered:

> When I arrived I found the place rather dull, a feeling of sadness around it - but then maybe that was just me, because I was sad inside. I sat there criticising the sombre décor and the dullness of the place to myself.
>
> About five minutes later this young woman came in. I realised that her whole demeanour was in fact the complete opposite of mine. Who was she? I was struck by a harmony about her which was even reflected in her dress. As people were arriving and we were waiting for the start of the day, I sat and watched her.
>
> Then the church opened for us to go to Mass. Again, in the church, I kept looking at her. Something was touching me deeply. I felt that there was some sort of mystical reality present in that young woman. Her

whole manner of being at the Mass fascinated me. I wanted to know her.

After the Mass we went back into a room in the Capuchin school where the priest was going to speak. He introduced the day and then he called on this young woman to speak. I was delighted. She spoke about love. That was just my problem! Everything in my life had led me to conclude that you couldn't really, fully, love on this earth.

She began, "There are many beautiful things on this earth... but the most beautiful is love."

She spoke of all the different expressions of love. Then she asked us that if we can know and experience this here on earth, what then would the love of God in Heaven be like?

Transported to the Heart of God

I was transported. I felt as if I was being lifted up - right into the heart of God. Everything in my life was being turned upside down and a great love of God was being awakened in me.

I'm sure that this wasn't just a feeling of great joy, but really was a divine experience. I knew there and then that this was my "way". I knew that it wouldn't just be a "flash in the pan" but would be lasting, the path of my life.

The next day, on the telephone, Natalia got Chiara's address from the priest. She wrote to her and Chiara responded, suggesting that Natalia call by the Capuchin school some day.

"Well, my heart was pounding as I rang the doorbell," recalled Natalia many years later, "and Chiara opened the door with such an expression of love, and greeted me as if she had always known me, that all my fears just melted away. She was wearing the pinafore that teachers of the time used to wear."

It was playtime for the children, and Chiara told me to stay with her for a while to have a chat. Although she was completely available to me, I could see that she was still attentive to the children running around. As different children would come up to her to show her something, or ask a question, or just for a hug, you could see that she loved each one of them equally.

She asked me about my life and told me about hers. She gave me her testimony - God is love. I could see that she lived that. She was indeed what she spoke of. I told her that her talk the previous Sunday had changed my life. Chiara replied, "Yes, of course. God is love."

"We won't preach, we'll live it"

I asked her why she could not teach this to the whole world. "Yes," she said, "the world is waiting. We won't preach it - we have to witness to it. If we can live this moment by moment, if we can live like Jesus would live, the world will believe."

"Since then," Natalia told this writer, "my path has been to follow Chiara unreservedly."

Natalia died quietly a few days after the funeral of Chiara in 2008.

Back then in 1943 she was one of Chiara's first "companions" or followers. Another was a young girl whose parents had asked Chiara to tutor in preparation for her university entrance exams.

Dori Zambonini was nervous and didn't think she could pass the exams. "Of course you will," encouraged Chiara. "We'll go to university together." Chiara's studies at the University of Venice were on hold as everything had come to a standstill because of the war. However, Dori's tuition continued. One day Chiara was expounding to her the philosophy of Immanuel Kant. Chiara seemed keen on Kant's thought and her enthusiasm was rubbing off on Dori. "Suddenly though," Dori recounted later, "my teacher stopped abruptly."

"Our Christianity," she said with feeling, "our faith, can't be reduced to science and physics. We are also citizens, in the early stages, of a world which is unknown to the empirical world of mechanical necessity. We are part of that world not only with our souls but also with our bodies. What about the resurrection? In what we've just been reading there is no place for the resurrection of the body!" After a short pause in which she reflected intently, she announced, "Come on; let's recite the Creed."

That "Come on" jolted Dori and the two young women stood up and recited the Creed, all the while touching the picture of the Sacred Heart on the wall in that room in Dori's home. They pronounced the phrase, "I believe in the resurrection of the body" with special emphasis.

This is the Ideal

When they sat down again Chiara began to explain the resurrection of the body.

"She explained it not only in a way that I had never heard before," recalled Dori, "but in such an irrefutable, actual and logical manner that I instinctively pinched both my arms to see if I was still in my body or whether I had left it. We both had the impression that a ray of light was shining on us from somewhere, perhaps from that picture of the Sacred Heart. It was a light that Chiara had translated into words, and which she summed up by saying, 'This is the Ideal'."

From then on the women would call the light that had been lit within them, which led them and guided their lives and the life which it produced in them and around them, "the Ideal".

The increasing number of young women who were drawn to Chiara were living through the worst days of the Second World War for the city of Trent. From one moment to the next they could see their homes destroyed, their friends and loved ones annihilated. They came to realise that there had to be more to life, something permanent, transcendent even; their Ideal; God.

In the spring of 1944, Natalia and Dori received permission to follow in the path of Chiara and make a private vow of perpetual virginity and dedication to Almighty God. They were the first of what would become a seemingly endless stream over the years and decades; indeed a whole host of virgins just as Chiara had foreseen in the basilica of Loreto.

Many other girls, sometimes pairs of sisters from the same family, were drawn to follow the "Ideal" of Chiara and her companions. As the air-raid sirens in Trent sounded, the women would run to the air-raid shelters taking with them only their copies of the New Testament and a torch. There, together, they would study a "word" from Our Lord to his disciples.

Creating Unity

One day in the dark cellar under Natalia's home, the companions were reading the Gospel by candle-light. They came across Our Lord's great priestly prayer on the night before his Passion. Chapter seventeen of St John's Gospel recounts how the Saviour prayed for his disciples, "May they be one Father, as we are one…."

This search to answer, or to live, the Lord's prayer for unity became a central guiding pillar of their Ideal. They learned that it was not just enough somehow to "wish" for this unity, but they had to live it. Thus they practised *being one,* or *becoming one*; being one in Christ as he and the Father are one. They came to term it "creating unity", or making themselves one with Christ and one with each other. Unfortunately, this aspect of Our Lord's Gospel seemed to have been somewhat neglected, or not overtly understood in recent times. In those days and in that place, the Communists had appropriated the call to "Unity". In fact, Chiara's brother Gino, his medical studies interrupted by the war, had become a communist activist and later became a journalist on the Communist Party's newspaper, *Unity*.

Jesus Forsaken

A few months before this discovery of the call to be one, in January of 1944, Dori was ill and Chiara was visiting her at her home. Just then a priest friend of theirs also came to call. During the course of their spiritual conversation the priest asked the two women if they knew when Jesus suffered the most. As they had been taught, they replied that it was surely Our Lord's agony in the garden of Gethsemane, when he knew what lay ahead of him and, being God, could even see the ingratitude with which his supreme sacrifice would be met by sinners down the ages.

> "No," replied the priest. "Our Lord's greatest suffering was when he was (apparently) totally abandoned by his Father and would even cry out on the cross, "My God, my God, why have you forsaken me?"

The women were stupefied. The very Son of God experienced being abandoned by God the Father; all for love of us, to accomplish our salvation. From that moment on Chiara and the ever-growing group of young women would do everything for *Jesus Forsaken*. Indeed, being part of the Body of Christ, they would somehow live in *Jesus Abandoned*.

From then until the very day she died, Chiara kept a picture of the Forsaken Jesus by her bedside, either beside her bed, or later on a large painting at the foot of her bed. It was the first thing she (and likewise all her "followers" in their homes) would see when they opened their eyes. Her, and their, first words on opening their eyes in the morning would be "Because you are forsaken".

Mary, Desolate Mother

Likewise, in pretty short order, they came to understand that Mary, Mother of Jesus (whom the Second Vatican Council would solemnly proclaim Mother of the Church) lived her vocation as *Mater Dei* and *Mater Ecclesiae* precisely at that moment when she seemingly *lost* her motherhood. She who stood at the foot of the cross did not flee as so many others, but gave up her Son to the Father. Our Lord even gifted her to the beloved disciple John (and by extension to all of us) from the cross, "Behold thy mother." In the moment when the lifeless body of the Saviour of the World was taken from the cross and laid on his mother's knees (as so poignantly depicted in Michelangelo's *Pietà* and countless artworks through the ages), in that moment, the Desolate One, the *Desolata*, was never *more so* mother of Christ and mother of humanity. Thus Chiara (and all the hundreds of thousands who have followed her "way" ever since) henceforth had those two pictures by their bedside: Jesus Forsaken and the Desolata.

As the war entered its final year, Trent came under heavier aerial bombardment, a target for both sides. On the 13th May 1944 there was a ferocious air-raid. The Lubich family fled into the hills, where they were eventually taken in by a pair of elderly sisters. But that first night, in the open air and seeing the bombs falling on their home town, Chiara wept. By now, many girls and young women were following her and her "way". Many were the poor whom they were providing for. She and some of her first companions had decided that whatever happened, they would not leave the city, but would stay - together, and with the poor.

The Little House

Chiara wept bitter tears as she realised that this would be a real wrench from her family. The next morning as daylight broke, and they all looked down at the city and saw their home destroyed, she broke the news. She would not continue with her parents and younger sisters into the mountains. She was going back down into the city. Her mother was heartbroken. To Chiara's surprise, though, her father seemed to understand and actually gave her his blessing.

Chiara was offered a little two-bedroom dwelling, 2 Piazza Cappucini, on the edge of Trent and she and Natalia moved in there, very soon joined by three other of the "first companions". Chiara named the humble residence the *Little House* in reference to the little Holy House at Loreto. The others went out to work each day and Chiara became the housekeeper. They continued to study the Gospels. Each "word" of the Lord became a new discovery, an adventure to be lived.

"Anyone who leaves father or mother for my sake shall be repaid a hundredfold." They seemed to experience this and as their every need seemed to be met, they simply referred to it in shorthand as "the hundredfold".

Anything in my name

"When two of you agree to ask the Father for anything in my name, it shall be given to you. …Whatsoever you do unto the least of my brethren you do unto me." As people could literally lose everything in seconds as their homes were bombed, the women came across many who were in need. So they might say a prayer, "Lord, you need a pair of shoes, size nine" and they would find that someone had dropped off just such a pair of shoes outside their house.

As the townspeople could see day in and day out that these women were caring for the poor, soon the Little House became like a goods depot. Food would arrive, clothing, bedding, shoes…And as the air-raids continued, the women were a common sight in the shelters. They could be easily recognised, always together, and each with her New Testament. And anyone arriving at the Little House at meal-times would see each woman at table with her poor person; a *focolarina*, a poor person, a *focolarina*, a poor person…

Communists? Or Protestants?

Of course, they were extraordinary times. Yet still Chiara and her first companions' response to the Gospel was radical, but not everyone immediately understood. This was 1940s Italy. Normally a girl left home only to get married, or else to enter a convent. Here was a group of them living together. Talking about unity! Were they communists? And reading the Scriptures! Were they Protestants? Complaints were made to the parish priests in the area, even to the bishop.

One of the Capuchin priests advised Chiara that she should begin to formulate a name for themselves, her "group", and think about a "rule of life" and so on. Such thoughts had never entered their minds. As far as they were concerned, they were merely Christians living the Christian Gospel.

"Who hears you..."

One of those "words" of the Lord they discovered was said to his apostles: "Who hears you, hears me... Whose sins you forgive they are forgiven..."

Chiara went to see the chief pastor - the local Ordinary - of Trent, Archbishop Carlo De Ferrari. She repeated many times throughout her life that if he had told her to stop what she was doing, she and her companions would have stopped immediately and returned to their families. "Who hears you hears me."

The archbishop received her like a father and at the end of their meeting gave his judgement, "Digitus Dei hic est". In other words, "this is God's work, God's hand is here." The archbishop was a friend and protector to the budding "movement" right up to his death in 1962.

Throughout her life Chiara wrote a monthly meditation on a word of Scripture. Every month for the rest of her life, she submitted that meditation to the Archbishop of Trent for approval before publishing it.

But in those early days, news of these young women was spreading like wildfire. When asked for a name of their group, Chiara said they were merely Christians trying to live in unity like the Holy Family. They became known as the *focolarine*, that is, those who gathered around the hearth. The group and later the large movement became, and is still nicknamed, the *Focolare*, that is the fireside, the hearth of a home.

The "Movement" Spreads

News of the archbishop's approval meant that they began to receive invitations from all around the archdiocese and the region to go and speak and share their experiences. Chiara could not be everywhere. From the start, she understood that building the unity the Lord desired meant using every means at one's disposal. It meant including those who were separated by distance due to work or illness and so she used the means of communication open to her: letters. She wrote copiously - as a means of "creating unity". She told the young women, though, that they could read her letters and meditations, but then they should destroy them. In order to be authentic witnesses, they should make the message their own.

As they criss-crossed the region, invited to speak in parish halls or private salons in towns and villages, whenever they passed by a hamlet, town or conurbation by train, they would seek out the church spire and gaze at it until out of sight, endeavouring in some way to unite themselves with Jesus present in the Blessed Sacrament in that church.

In 1947, the first men's *focolare* opened in Trent. The brother of two of the young women, Marco Tecilla, was doing some electrical work in the Little House and was taken by the atmosphere of unity and harmony there. Soon, he requested to live like them and he and a friend went to see the archbishop. He gave them approval to go ahead. Their first dwelling was a converted chicken coop.

Marco was not the first young man to have visited the Little House. In May of 1945 two young men, Communist activists, came to visit. They said to Chiara, "We've been watching you and your companions, how you care for the poor and try to create unity. But we, the Communists, we will be the ones to build that united society." Chiara didn't argue with them. She pointed to the crucifix on the wall and then merely said, "Let's see who gets there first then."

As we saw, Gino Lubich had become an ardent communist and worked on the Party's newspaper, *Unity*. In the following years, he saw and came to understand the work begun by his sister. He reconverted to Catholicism and worked on the magazine and publishing house which had then been started up by the Focolare. At the Mass in December 1943 where Chiara consecrated herself to God by a private vow, the "special intention" she had written to be placed under the chalice was, "For the conversion of my brother Gino".

With the official approval of the archbishop, the end of the war and the increasing ability to travel again, the first companions of Chiara were able to criss-cross the region and even respond to invitations from further afield.

A couple of them had spoken to private gatherings in Rome and soon the invitations to Chiara herself to visit the Eternal City became more pressing. Archbishop De Ferrari was a member of a religious congregation called the Order of the Sacred Stigmata. He put Chiara in touch with a Fr Tomassi who had been the superior general of that order.

Invitation to Rome

With Graziella De Lucca and others of her first companions, Chiara met many nuns and priests who were interested to hear about her living of the Gospel. Some of the Roman Papal nobility also arranged gatherings in their palazzos and Graziella would give her testimony to those too. Soon parish priests invited her to speak in their parish halls. Then, the Vicar Apostolic of Rome (that is, the bishop designated by the Pope to run his diocese of Rome) invited her to speak to various Church gatherings.

In March of 1948 Chiara received a letter from a young Franciscan friar who was studying in Rome. He must have been able instinctively to understand more of the Focolare's message than most at that time. For the most part, the first companions perhaps focused on testifying to God's love and how it could be lived and experienced here on earth, and on Our Lord's priestly prayer to the Father, "May they be one as we are one…" Yet this young Franciscan, Brother Jerome, seems to have understood that all of that is based, grows from, Christ's total abandonment to the Father, even to the Lord himself having experienced that forsakenness.

In her letter of reply to Brother Jerome, Chiara wrote,

> My God, my God, why have you forsaken me?
> My dear brother in Jesus,
> As soon as I received your letter, I went straight into town. Jesus had to be the first and last witness to the joy that filled my soul. [She meant that she went straight to the Eucharistic presence of Jesus reserved in the tabernacle of the church.]
>
> It could only be thus. I am convinced that unity in its most spiritual, most intimate, most profound aspect cannot be understood except by the souls who have chosen as their portion in life Jesus Forsaken who cries out, "My God, my God, why have you forsaken me?"
>
> Brother, now that I have found in you an understanding of what the secret of unity is, I would like, and could, speak to you for days on end! I want you to know that Jesus Forsaken is everything. He is the guarantee of unity. All light on unity flows forth from that cry [of Jesus on the cross].
>
> To choose him as the one aim, the one goal, the destination of your life is to bring countless other people into unity. The book of light which the Lord is writing on my soul has two aspects: a page shining with mysterious love: Unity. A page glowing with mysterious suffering: Jesus Forsaken. They are two sides of the same coin.

The page of Unity is for everyone. For me and for all those in the front line of Unity, Jesus Forsaken is our everything.

Wanting to instruct a future apostle of unity built on Jesus Forsaken, she gave him many instructions on where to seek out the Abandoned Jesus (in sinners, our brothers who are without God) and concludes her letter:

Dear Brother, not everyone understands these words. We must treasure them so that Love, Forsaken Love, may be surrounded by hearts which understand him because they have glimpsed him in their lives and have seen in him the answer to everything.

For the others Unity, and for us the abandonment. Yes, because the bride cannot be different from the bridegroom.

Jesus is without God. To console him, let us promise him that he will always find Jesus amongst us. "Where two or more... there am I." Jesus will console Jesus who cries out. "My Jesus! Our Jesus!"

Chiara of Jesus Forsaken.

Igino Giordani

In September 1948 some of Chiara's collaborators in Rome invited her to come with them to meet a renowned parliamentarian, a deputy (MP) in the Italian parliament, who represented the constituency of Roma-Tivoli.

Igino Giordani, wounded in the Great War, had gone on to become a linguist, a well-known writer and renowned librarian. He had spent a year in Washington DC studying the system of classification used in the Library of Congress. When he was made Director of the Vatican Library he overhauled it with this new system. He also founded the Vatican's renowned School of Librarianship.

In his lifetime Giordani wrote some ninety-four books. He also translated nine other major works into Italian. He wrote in forty-two different newspapers and reviews. Much of his early works concerned the Church Fathers and lives of the saints. He also wrote two major works on the Social Teaching of the Church, which remain on the reading-list of many seminaries to this day. He was a great expert on, having written two major books about, St Catherine of Siena, the great Italian saint who (together with St Teresa of Avila) in 1970 became one of the first two female Doctors of the Church.

By now Chiara was persuaded by friends and companions that the burgeoning movement needed a permanent presence there in Rome, at the heart of the Church. One of the reasons she had agreed to meet this deputy for Rome was that she was in need of a property to that end. In fact, Giordani did find a property for the growing "movement" in Rome. He also asked Chiara to write down for him what she was working for, a sort of outline of her "Ideal" of unity. Using this as a basis, he wrote a long article about the movement in *Fides*, a monthly review for which he wrote regularly.

Voice of Mystical Experience

In his memoirs, published in 1981, Giordani wrote of his first encounter with this young woman come down to Rome from Trent: "Exercising the courtesy of an MP meeting possible electors, I met in Parliament one day a group of religious. They represented the different Franciscan families and with them were a layman and a young laywoman."

The first thing that struck the busy MP who was well-versed in Church affairs was the fact that these various branches of Franciscans were all acting together and in harmony. That he considered a miracle, and he told them so.

Then, he says, the young woman began to speak:

> I was expecting to hear the sentimental propaganda of some utopian voluntary association. Quite the contrary. From her very first words, I could see that there was something new here. In her voice there was an unusual timbre; the timbre of a deep and sure conviction which came from mystical experience.

His perception of the twenty-eight-year-old Chiara at that first meeting was that she was someone "who put holiness within reach of everyone. She tore down the grille which separated the world of the laity from the mystical life. She rendered God near, she caused people to discover him as father, brother, friend, present to humanity."

For her part, Chiara was completely unaware of the gigantic impression that their first meeting had made on the respected writer and MP. She later remembered,

> It was just a simple meeting. I wasn't aware of the impact it had on Giordani. I only learned something of that afterwards when he sent a letter to me in Trent. In it he spoke of Jesus's last Testament in such a clear and profound way that I began to think that he was someone who had been put on our path by God.

Co-Founder

Indeed, Chiara and Giordani would become close collaborators in seeking the will of God for the rest of Giordani's life. Chiara would come to call him a co-founder of the Focolare Movement.

So far, those following in Chiara's wake in total consecration to God had been young women, then young men, committing to a life of perpetual virginity. Giordani, the great expert on the famous saint, had already described Chiara to his friends and parliamentary colleagues as "a second St Catherine of Siena". He was completely inspired by his contact with Chiara and came to look on this young woman almost half his age as a "spiritual mother, a guide and sister".

Giordani had once written that "in the Church's calendar of feasts [at that time] there is not even one married couple of saints". Now, this grand intellectual, married to Mya with whom he had four children, felt inspired by this call to holiness in embracing Jesus Forsaken. Through all the usual means of discernment and obedience to the Church authorities, Igino Giordani became the first married *focolarino*.

After his death in 1980, and when his official Cause for Beatification was opened, his remains were transferred to a tomb in the chapel of the Focolare Movement's headquarters outside Rome. As we have read, Chiara's remains were laid to rest there after her funeral in March 2008. In June 2015 the first *focolarino* to be ordained a priest, Don Pasquale Foresi, died and was buried in the remaining third tomb. Thus Chiara and her two "co-founders" are all now buried in the Centre of the Focolare.

By January 1949, Chiara was living full-time in Rome. She and some of her first companions formed a *focolare* in a flat made available to them. Later, her parents would also move there and live in another flat in the same building as their daughter. Both would live out their days, and die, at the heart of the movement, near to their beloved daughter.

From the City to the Mountains and back

In the summer of 1949 Chiara, along with many of her first companions and hundreds of "followers of the Ideal" went to spend some holiday time in Tonadico in the Dolomite mountains. Gathered around Chiara, they were to have a formative experience which would affect the future shape and direction of the ever-growing "movement". During those days spent in the clean pure air of the northern Italian mountains, Chiara had a series of intuitions or insights. They were to do with the new *spirituality of communion* which was emerging among them. She shared everything that happened to her and that she "intuited" with those who were with her, and with others who were absent - such as Natalia who had had to return to work in Trent - via letter.

Paradise '49

These experiences of Chiara and those around her came to be known as "Paradise '49". They sprang from the mystical experience which she and her first companions had had of what happens when Christians take seriously Jesus's New Commandment to "love one another has I have loved you", and when their nourishment is the Eucharist, the bond of unity.

Chiara with her parents Luigi and Luigia in the Italian Dolomites during a summer Mariapolis in the early 1950s. In earlier times the young Lubich family had holidayed there.

In a sense it was about identifying oneself (while retaining the distinction, of course) with Jesus himself, who is present in the heart of the Father. It is as St Augustine wrote in his *Confessions* about the words heard on high regarding the Eucharist: "You shall not transform me into yourself, but you will be transformed into me" (*Confessions* VII.10.16).

So, in those days in the mountains, just five and a half years after Chiara had made her own consecration to God, and five years since Natalia and Dori had been the first ones to follow suit, the future make-up of what would become a world-wide movement was being made clear. There would be communities of consecrated virgins, women and men, as well as married people who would also live in total consecration to God according to their state in life. Later in that same year (at a Christmas get-together in Trent) Chiara confirmed the desire of a young male Focolare adherent, Pasquale Foresi, for the priesthood. In the future, priests, monks, friars, religious sisters and even bishops would be able to become members of this movement.

"Paradise '49" was thus a founding experience which set the path for the future of this movement which would come to be present in every area of the Church and in every part of the globe.

"Come off the mountain"

Igino Giordani, the first married person in the movement, was central to this. As the heavenly atmosphere did not diminish and Chiara seemed to experience fresh lights to communicate to her companions every day, it seemed like a foretaste of heaven. Who would want to leave such an atmosphere and such an experience?

It fell to Giordani to tell Chiara that she must "come down off the mountain". One day he told her, "You have to come back down to the world. You have many children whom you must lead to God."

"I have only one Spouse"

In silence, Chiara acknowledged that what he said was true. She knew it in her heart - but the very thought of voluntarily leaving this veritable foretaste of heaven was heartrending for her. She asked Giordani for some paper. Then she left him, went to her room and through her tears (on Chamber of Deputies notepaper!) poured out her heart in writing:

> I have only one Spouse on earth: Jesus crucified and forsaken.
> I have no other God but him.
> In him there is the whole of paradise with the Trinity and the whole of earth with humanity.
> Therefore what is his is mine, and nothing else.

And his is universal suffering, and therefore mine.
I will go through the world seeking it
in every instant of my life.
What hurts me is mine.
Mine the suffering that grazes me in the present.
Mine the suffering of the souls beside me.
Mine all that is not peace, not joy,
not beautiful, not lovable, not serene…
So it will be for the years I have left:
a thirst for suffering, anguish, despair,
separation, exile, forsakenness, torment,
for…all that is him
and he is suffering.
In this way I will dry up the waters of tribulation in
many hearts nearby,
and through communion with my almighty Spouse,
in many far away.
I shall pass as a fire
that consumes all that must fall
and leaves standing only the truth.

Over Christmas of 1949, Chiara returned to Trent for a reunion of many of the first companions. There were now several female *focolares* or households in Trent and those who travelled up with Chiara were lodged in these houses. Some of the men involved in Rome also came and they were lodged with families involved with the movement. One young man who had been invited along to the reunion, and who squeezed in along with so many others into the living-room of one of the female *focolares* to hear Chiara on that Christmas Eve was the twenty year-old Pasquale Foresi.

Earlier that year he had met Graziella De Lucca, one of Chiara's first companions. Graziella had been invited to Pistoia by the local MP to address a meeting that he and a local priest had organised. That MP was Pasquale's father.

Pasquale had already spent two years studying philosophy at his local seminary before being sent to Rome. While there he experienced a crisis of faith and left the seminary. He offered to accompany Graziella to the meeting and as they walked through the market square he asked her, "What exactly are you and your friends trying to achieve?"

Her reply, he later recounted, was frank and crystal clear: "We want to relive the Trinity on earth". Pasquale was astounded. Here was this young woman speaking of mysteries which he had spent so long studying in his theological classes. She and her friends were bringing it into the arena of everyday human life and experience. He soaked up everything that Graziella said during that conversation and during the meeting which followed.

Graziella arranged to stay on for another day and to meet the young man again. They spoke for seven hours. Pasquale recalled that among the myriad questions he put to her was, "What do you think about the Eucharist? Graziella knew nothing of the crisis the young man had been through regarding the priesthood. She answered him, "For us it is so important that we couldn't even imagine a single day without receiving Holy Communion."

No Christ without Church

"Her answer hit me like a ton of bricks," recalled Pasquale, "because in that instant I understood that in order to have the Eucharist you had to have the priesthood, the hierarchy. I understood then that you could not separate the Church from Christ. I realised also that we are all Church. It was not 'the Church' that had to change, or 'the others' that had to change. *I* had to change. *I* had to start a new life."

There that Christmas Eve, in the tiny little sitting-room, Pasquale found himself in close quarters with Chiara: he was squeezed into a seat right next to her at the head of the table!

Chiara began to share with the assembled company the very particular experience that she had lived that summer with others of the movement up in Tonadico. Others there that night remembered that a very special atmosphere seemed to surround them all as Chiara recounted her experiences. Pasquale said later, "There was such warmth in what she was saying in that completely clear, transparent way of hers that my heart and mind felt completely full. I can't remember the exact words that she actually said, but it would be no exaggeration to say that I felt I was in heaven."

Then Chiara began to ask the others what they thought about what she had just shared. Pasquale remembers being terrified that she might ask him. "If I say the wrong thing," he thought, "I'll ruin this beautiful atmosphere".

Reality of the Mystical Body

Just then Chiara looked straight at him and said, "And you, what do you think?"

Pasquale surprised even himself when he replied, "In this Ideal I see the reality of the Mystical Body of Christ being realised".

A few days later, in early January of 1950, he left for Rome on the same train as Chiara and her group. There he lodged with a family, ate his midday meal at the friary of a religious friend, and spent as much time as he could at the *focolare* of Chiara (who was then living in a small apartment with Graziella and two other early companions). Then he realised that as he was not yet twenty-one, he needed to go home and obtain permission from his parents to move permanently to Rome and live in a *focolare*. His plan was to live in the *focolare* and work in a factory.

When he returned, Chiara and her household had moved to the port town of Ostia where a house had been made available to them. Pasquale would travel out from Rome to visit them whenever he could. One day he was walking through the hallway of the house when Chiara, with a broom in her hands, suddenly stopped him and asked, "What would you think about sharing with me the burden of responsibility for the movement?" Somewhat dumbstruck he nodded his head in acceptance!

First *Focolarino* Priest

During the group's next summer holiday in Tonadico in the mountains, in September of that year 1950, Chiara approached Pasquale after Mass one day and said, "I've got something to tell you but first I want to know if you have already understood it yourself."

Until then, the movement was entirely made up of lay people and was seen and understood by them all to be a specifically lay movement, after the fashion of Chiara's "fourth way".

"After a moment's hesitation," recalled Pasquale, "I told her exactly how I felt; of the certainty growing within me that I should be a priest."

"That's exactly what I wanted to tell you," said Chiara.

Pasquale took up his studies again at Rome's Pontifical Gregorian University. Four years later, on 3rd April 1954, in the cathedral of Trent, Archbishop De Ferrari ordained him to the priesthood.

Already in 1951 Chiara had entrusted Pasquale with responsibility for all the men's households in the movement. When official approval of the movement came from the Holy See in 1962, Fr Pasquale helped Chiara to write the first set of statutes for the movement which would be submitted to and accepted by the Universal Church.

But there would be a lot of trials and tribulations to be gone through before arriving at that point.

Marian Year

The year Fr Foresi was ordained, 1954, had been declared by Pope Pius XII to be a Marian Year. In that year, also, Chiara made a pilgrimage to Fatima, along with her "co-founder" Igino Giordani and a rather special friend who was the important link that allowed what happened there. For Chiara and Igino, along with Elena Rossignani, had a private meeting with the one surviving visionary of Fatima, Sr Lucia. Elena was the niece of Pope Pius XII; her mother, the Marchese Pacelli in Rossignani, was the Pope's sister.

The Marchese Pacelli attended some of the summer gatherings of the Focolare Movement in the 1950s. At one stage, before the ever-growing movement had a permanent headquarters, the marchese had put at their disposal the Villa Pacelli in the hills outside Rome. At the meeting in Sr Lucia's convent, in the parlour with the three visitors on one side and the enclosed Carmelite nun on the other side of the grille, Chiara told her all about the work of the Holy Spirit in the movement, how they tried to live and attain Christ's last prayer, "That they may be one, Father", and the effect this was having on so many people who were living as Christian sisters and brothers in mutual charity.

Sr Lucia: more work to do

Sr Lucia listened intensely. Chiara recalled in writing some years later, "At the end of our meeting Lucia spoke to us like a dear sister. She promised to pray for us and for our work and her gaze never left us until we exited the room." In fact, throughout the rest of Sr Lucia's life (she died in 2005) she and Chiara remained united in prayer and in occasional contact by letter. When in the early 1990s Chiara suffered a bout of ill-health and was holed up in the house given to her and the movement by a benefactor in the Swiss Alps, Sr Lucia sent her a message. The Seer of Fatima told her that she should leave Switzerland and return to her movement's headquarters outside Rome. There was a lot more work for her yet to do, said Lucia.

Back in the 1950s though, Chiara's encounter with Pope Pius XII was not because the Pope's sister was involved with Focolare.

In 1951, a twenty-five-year-old business studies graduate called Giulia Folonari met one of Chiara's first companions, Valeria Ronchetti. So struck was she by Valeria's witness of how she and her friends in Trent were trying to live the Gospel one phrase at a time, that a few days later she turned up unannounced in Trent. When she got to 2 Piazza Cappucini there was no one at home. In fact, it was the very day that that Focolare household was moving out of the Little House to another residence.

Struck by Chiara's "look"

Giulia was the eldest of eight siblings, part of a grand family and producers of the famous Folonari wine. That summer, it happened that the Folonaris were holidaying in a village in the Dolomites not far from Tonadico where Chiara and the *focolarine* were. Giulia twice made the journey over to Tonadico. She recounted once to this writer her first encounter with Chiara. It was in the street. Another *focolarina* introduced her and Chiara simply greeted her before continuing on her way. But the "look" of Chiara struck Giulia. She recalled how there and then she was reminded of the Gospel phrase which says of the rich young man that "Jesus looked on him and loved him" (*Mk* 10:21). "I didn't say a word," recalled Giulia. "I was just struck to the core by this look of love which came from her."

After the summer holidays, in September 1951, Giulia could no longer resist the draw. She felt irresistibly attracted to live the way Chiara and those other young women around her lived. She told her parents. Her mother said, "Yes, of course, dear, but you don't have to go to Rome to live the Gospel!" Her father, though, gave his implicit blessing. As the eldest of his children, he gave Giulia an errand to accomplish with a bank in Rome, and the next day she went. Once again, she turned up at a *focolare* unannounced; except, this time, she never left.

Chiara in the early 1950s. This was about the time (1954) that she met privately with Sr Lucia of Fatima at her convent in Portugal. She was under thorough investigation by Church authorities and also being purified in the Dark Night of the Soul.

She became known as "Eli" in the movement (after Our Lord's cry of abandonment "Eli, Eli, lama sabachthani…") and for the next fifty-seven years never left Chiara's side. She was with her literally until Chiara's dying breath (except, that is, for a few months when Chiara entrusted Eli with establishing a *focolare* in Jerusalem and another in Belgium). Eli became Chiara's secretary and driver and was, perhaps more than anyone, privy to her most private thoughts, emotions, trials and joys.

Another Day, Another Soul

Well, in those days in the early 1950s, Chiara used to encourage her companions, spiritual children, sisters and brothers (whatever they felt themselves to be) never to let a day pass without reaching out to another soul.

While researching the story of Chiara's life and her movement, this writer worked closely with Eli Folonari. She recounted how Chiara's watchword of the time was *nulla dies sine anima*, never a day without another soul. "I wanted to follow this advice too," she remembered, "but I had just arrived in Rome and didn't know anyone. Ah! But then I remembered that there was at least a 'contact' who worked in the Vatican. He was the brother of my uncle by marriage and I had only met him once at a family wedding."

That "contact" was Monsignor Montini. His family, like Eli's, was from Brescia and his brother had married Eli's aunt. Undaunted, she telephoned Montini's office to say, "Hi. I'm in Rome now. Perhaps we could meet sometime?" He immediately invited his young countrywoman to visit him in his office in the Vatican. Eli had her first "soul" to witness to about the graces of the Ideal.

Montini, who was at that time National Chaplain to Catholic students, later became Pius's Under-Secretary of State, and then Archbishop of Milan before being elected to the Papacy to succeed Pope St John XXIII.

First Papal Audience

Anyway, Monsignor Montini obtained an audience of Pope Pius XII for Chiara and some of the first *focolarine* (the women) and *focolarini* (the men). Chiara later recalled that when they were presented to the Pope, he immediately showed that he knew of them. "Ah, the *focolarini!* Good, good! Where's the leader?" Eli remembers that they never used that word, and wouldn't dare to. She pointed out Chiara and presented her as their "initiator".

Chiara recounted,

He turned towards me with a really genuine and paternal friendliness. He wanted to know about each one of us, what we did and where we came from. I explained to him that we represented different parts of Italy where the Movement was present. He was particularly interested in Tuscany and Emilia, explaining that in those regions where Communism dominated, you could sense more strongly the influence of materialism. One of us replied, "We want to bring Jesus to the world. Each one of us has hundreds of souls behind her, and we follow each one of them personally… We want to be the joy of the Church."

"And the Church needs it so much," replied the Pope. "Continue your work. Go forward!" At the end he gave us a solemn blessing, and as he was being led away to his next appointment, he kept looking back and waving to us.

That was Chiara's first personal contact with a pope. As Pope Benedict said in his funeral message, she had close contact with each and every pope thereafter. *Ubi Petrus, ibi ecclesia*: "Where Peter is, there is the Church"; and Chiara's overwhelming desire was to be united with Christ's Vicar on Earth and to be of service to him. Every letter that she subsequently received from the Pope, she kept on her desk, always.

Of course, the most contact was had with the long-reigning Pope St John Paul II. He had known the work of the Focolare behind the Iron Curtain in the 1960s and 70s. When he was elected Pope in October 1978, he immediately had his secretary Mgr Stanisław Dziwisz telephone Eli and invite Chiara and her to his first private Mass in the Apostolic Palace the next morning.

Time of Trials and Doubts

But back in Rome of the 1950s, life was not quite so straightforward for Chiara. As a result of doubts and accusations, the Holy Office had launched a full investigation of this young woman and her work. It was a time of trial for Chiara, even though she understood what Mgr Montini explained: that this investigation by the Church authorities would ultimately be for her own protection, that ultimate approval would bring her and her movement under the protection of the Holy See itself. And so it would prove to be.

But in those early days there were all sorts of doubts. Regarding "the initiator" herself, who was she? Chiara's confessor and her bishop had confirmed to her that she had a charism, that is, a gift that was not for herself but for the good of the Church. That is why she immediately shared with her companions any insights, lights, joys or tribulations which she experienced.

There were accusations that young people were leaving home and family, even breaking off engagements, to join this young woman's movement. All this talk of "unity" - wasn't this communism in disguise? And all this reading of Scripture, wasn't that somewhat dangerous?

Various restrictions were put in place during those ten years of investigation. Chiara might not speak in public. For some time she could not even have contact with her young male *focolarini* who were studying for the priesthood. Eli remembered, half a century later, that Chiara was never actually called in to the Holy Office to be questioned. The officials always came to see her, at her residence. They always left in tears, moved by the simplicity, limpidity and evident holiness of this young woman.

Dark Night of the Soul

During this period, particularly in 1952, Chiara also appears to have undergone the "dark night of the soul", or so she was assured by a famous spiritual guide she consulted. This holy priest gave her the writings of St John of the Cross, which aided Chiara greatly. She always retained a great affinity for that saint as well as for St Teresa of Avila. On one of her last journeys outside Italy, Chiara visited St Teresa's convent at Toledo and was invited inside the enclosure by the Carmelite nuns. In the visitors' book she wrote, "St Teresa constructed the Interior Castle; we have been constructing the Exterior Castle. All in the Church, in the joy of the Communion of Saints".

As noted earlier, Chiara clung to her belief in the Lord's word to his apostles, "Who hears you, hears me." All her commentaries on sacred Scripture, even short meditations, she submitted to the Archbishop of Trent for his imprimatur.

Public Episcopal Support

In 1956, at the height of the accusations and investigations, the Archbishop of Trent published a statement making his position absolutely clear:

> To whom it may concern.
> What I think about the Focolare can be summed up in a few words. I witnessed its birth in my diocese and I have

always regarded it as an exceptional company of very fine souls whose lives were edifying in every respect. Their genuine spirit of charity and zealous sense of apostolate are sure proof that in this poor world, "set as it is on a course to ruin", there are still Christians who are able to scale the most demanding heights of virtue and mine the deepest recesses of goodness.

For twelve years now, I have been vigilant and attentive in my observation of them, and during that time, I have never had cause to reprove them. On the contrary, they have always been a joy, a rare experience for me in more than fifty years of pastoral ministry. I have already said this in the past. I have put it in writing on other occasions, and now I repeat it: would that there were legions of Focolarini!

Signed: Carlo De Ferrari, Archbishop.

Already, a couple of years earlier, the German Bishops' Conference had approved the movement.

Regarding the time of investigations and suspicions, Chiara later said,

It was a time of suffering for us. Until we received the official approval of the Pope, we passed through a period of suspense, uncertainty and forsakenness.

Several factors came to the fore for us during those years. First of all, a deep love of Jesus crucified and forsaken, which always sustained us. We had chosen him and now he was making himself known to us in grand style. It was an opportunity to prove our genuine love for him. Then there was our strong belief in the Church's maternity, which must have come to us directly from heaven. Finally, it was a period of extraordinary fruits. The movement, which had already spread to different parts of Europe, now began to reach other continents. We saw the beginning of its ecumenical work and its initial penetration of countries behind the Iron Curtain so as to help the Church in Eastern Europe. It was a time of blessings, immense blessings. "Unless the grain of wheat falls into the earth and dies, it remains alone; but if it dies, it bears much fruit" (*Jn* 12:24).

Pope Pius XII died in 1958. It turned out that he had left a note regarding the Focolare and his wish to see it officially approved. After discussion at the Italian Bishops' Conference in 1960, Pope St John XXIII appointed a papal commission to oversee the process of fully integrating the movement into the structures of the Church. Once the commission had completed its task, Pope St John XXIII officially and publicly approved the Focolare Movement on 23rd March 1962. All restrictions on its public activities were lifted.

From the earliest days, the young Don Foresi had assisted Chiara in drawing up statutes for recognition by the Church. As the Work, the movement, developed and expanded during the life of the foundress, this task was ongoing in order to enshrine the new realities addressed by the movement as it continually developed. An early example would be that of integrating married people into a full membership of what would become a multi-faceted movement. As time went on, areas or "branches" of the work would be set up to encompass young people and even children of various age-groups. Male *focolarini* would be allowed to become priests. Diocesan priests, even religious, would be allowed to become part of Focolare. Eventually, even bishops would have their own "branch" of the movement.

Lutherans and Anglicans

From the beginning of the 1960s, Chiara had met some Lutherans who attended a talk she gave in Germany. They wanted to become involved in this work too. Then, during the lead-up to the Second Vatican Council, she met a Canon Pawley of the Anglican Communion who was resident in Rome. He quickly arranged meetings for other non-Catholic Christians to encounter this woman and her work. Chiara also made the first of many visits to England. Whenever Chiara visited another country or region, her first official port of call would always be to the local Catholic Ordinary and often also the papal representative or nuncio in that area. But she was clear; the Ideal, this God-Love, Jesus Forsaken, was for everybody. Of course she, then, and her "followers" must also be for everybody.

As Anglicans and Lutherans and other Christians wanted to live this message as part of this movement, a way had to be found to incorporate their status into the statutes and so on. Chiara understood that constantly updating and developing these statutes and having them approved by the Church hierarchy was the guarantee and safeguard of the work's authenticity.

The movement itself is officially named in the statutes as *The Work of Mary*. As that daily prayer of Chiara and all the *focolarini* stated, their aim was and is to be in some way a presence of Mary in the Church.

Always a Woman Leader

One day in 1990 when the latest version of the statutes was being developed for submission and approval, Chiara mentioned to Pope St John Paul II that some members of her Council had wondered whether it might not be possible to state therein that the President of the Work should always be a woman. The Polish pope did not hesitate: No, it was not a question of *may* always be a woman, but the President of the Work of Mary *must* always be a woman! He went on to explain to her the different "profiles" of the Church, in particular the Petrine and the Marian profiles, the hierarchical structural side which is necessary for teaching, for administration of the sacraments and so on; but also the Marian profile. Indeed, the Second Vatican Council had (as we remarked) solemnly defined Mary as Mother of the Church.

Thus in this "Work of Mary" there could be various categories of "membership" or "adhesion" but all based around the "host of virgins" revealed to Chiara at Loreto all those years ago.

To facilitate the contacts with members of other Christian ecclesial communities, Chiara set up the *Centro Uno* in Rome in the 1960s. The Vatican Council, of course, brought so many bishops to Rome from all over the world and Chiara received invitations to establish *focolares* in many countries. With the spread of the movement to so many parts of the world, contacts began and increased with followers of other religions too. So today there are Jewish and Muslim adherents of the movement in several parts of the world.

Non-Christian Religions

During the Second Session of the Second Vatican Council, some people asked, in light of the success of the new Secretariat for Promoting Christian Unity, might it not now be appropriate to set up a secretariat for dialogue with the major non-Christian religions? Finally Pope Paul decided to do this; the only non-Christian guest invited to attend the Third Session of the Council was a Buddhist layman who in 1938 had founded a movement for Buddhist laypeople. In a similar fashion to Chiara's cornerstone of Our Lord's priestly prayer, so his movement was founded on a sacred Buddhist text. He and Chiara met when he was nominated for the Templeton Prize for Progress in Religion in 1979. He had read the speech that Chiara gave when she received that prize in 1977 and he travelled to Italy to meet her.

Everywhere there is Buddha

Four years later Chiara was in Tokyo. Her first calls were upon the local archbishop and the papal nuncio. As always, wherever she was, she shared her impressions with her fellow *focolarini*. Writing from the Far East she once wrote, "Everywhere there is Buddha, Buddha, Buddha… We who have Jesus present among us. How often do we neglect him?" She encouraged her consecrated *focolarini* who lived in community to increase their daily adoration of the Blessed Sacrament from one hour to two.

Twelve thousand leaders of the Buddhist movement mentioned above, called *Rissho Kosei-kai*, waited to welcome Chiara to Tokyo. The Great Sacred Hall of their movement's temple was full to capacity and an overspill followed proceedings from television link-ups in the foyer and the surrounding corridors. To a completely silent and attentive audience Chiara said,

> Today I have the honour of presenting my spiritual experience. Take it as a gift of love offered by your sister.
>
> As you certainly know, I am Christian and belong to the Catholic Church. The Catholic Church, which has been living in the world for twenty centuries, has as its principle aim the sanctification of people. It does this by means of the grace which Jesus brought on earth and which confers on men the dignity of the Sons of God.

She stressed that the Church cares about the whole person too, outlining the corporal works of mercy. What the Church has given the world in these centuries, only God could measure.

On several occasions Chiara was invited to give her Christian testimony to Buddhists in Japan and other Far Eastern countries.

The Catholic Church is one, is holy, is universal and is founded on the apostles chosen by Jesus. But if the Church is one and holy, the people who make it up, who live in the midst of the world, can sometimes be affected by the confusion and the negative influences which from time to time exist in humanity.

Charism as spiritual medicine

She went on to explain how God thus sends a sort of "spiritual medicine" via charisms necessary for a particular time "which strengthen the Christian community".

Chiara then shared with her rapt listeners her own story, from her consecration to God in 1943, to the experience of that group of first companions discovering the "words" of Scripture: "God is Love" (*1 Jn* 4:16); "No greater love …than to lay down your life for your friends" (*Jn* 15:13); "By this shall all men know you are my disciples, if you love one another" (*Jn* 13:35); "Give and it will be given to you" (*Lk* 6:38), and so on, until she came to the words, "Unless a grain of wheat dies…" Then she explained:

The members of the Movement know all this. They have experienced suffering, but also its beneficial effects. That much suffering has been loved is one of the causes of the rapid spread of the Movement throughout the world…

By way of purification by God, one can in fact enter little by little into contemplation of the things of God. Then we can understand something of his mysteries. And if the Christian in fact remains faithful to the message of love and suffering contained in the Gospel, he is led by the Spirit of God into a deeper unity with Christ, until he can say, "It is no longer I who live but Christ who lives in me" (*Ga* 2:20). So he becomes another Christ, in Christ, participating with him in his filial relationship with the Father.

Chiara told the twelve thousand Buddhist leaders that after forty years, the movement now existed among Catholics in almost every nation on earth, and for the past twenty years also among Christians of other ecclesial communities. She shared with them what a marvellous experience it was for her when she met members of other religions, for:

Every person, made in the image of God, has the possibility of a certain personal relationship with him. Moreover, the very nature of man brings him to this communion. This is the affinity we find in various ways between our religion and others.

From Japan, Chiara went on to visit the Focolare Movement in other Far Eastern countries and then landed in Manila, capital of the Philippines. While there she stayed in the movement's "little town" of Tagaytay and there inaugurated a study centre for members of her movement in Asia, dedicated to the study of Eastern religions.

Apart from the work of *Centro Uno* in Rome, the movement's "little town" of Ottmaring, near Augsburg in Germany, had become of a centre of life and dialogue between Catholics and other Christians.

Little Towns

The story of how the movement came to establish not only *focolares* which would be a model of that "little house" of Nazareth, but also "little towns" once again involves the unannounced arrival of Eli Folonari, who became Chiara's lifelong secretary and driver.

One day in 1961, during their annual summer stay in Switzerland, Eli had driven Chiara, as usual, for an afternoon break to get away from the relentless administrative work of the movement. They stopped the car and got out for a walk. As they came to the crest of a hill they paused to look down. There spread out below them was the little Swiss town of Einsiedeln. The town grew up around a very famous Benedictine abbey, and many visit the Marian shrine which it houses.

Chiara recounted,

> We looked down on the imposing structure of the abbey, with the beautiful church at its centre where the monks prayed, with the two wings where they lived and studied,

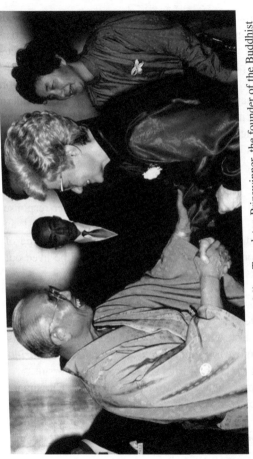

Chiara is welcomed in 1981 by fellow Templeton Prizewinner, the founder of the Buddhist Rissho Kosei-kai Movement at their headquarters in Tokyo. As she told them of Jesus and his Mystical Body on Earth, the Catholic Church, she asked them to accept this teaching "as a gift of love offered by your sister."

with the school building and the surrounding fields where they worked and raised livestock. It seemed to us that we were looking at the fulfilment of St Benedict's ideal: "pray and work".

With that splendid sight before us, another vision took shape in our hearts. It was the dream of a modern "little city" with houses, workshops, craft centres and industries where we could bear witness to our ideal of unity. It was a powerful intuition.

From then on, whenever people urged Chiara that her movement needed to have a "headquarters" in or around Rome like so many Catholic organisations, her response was always along the lines, "We don't need just an administrative headquarters building, we need a type of headquarters 'little city' where our ideal will be lived out in all facets of life!"

Property in Common

Shortly after Eli Folonari had come to Rome to join the Focolare, her brother Vincenzo received permission of his parents to move to Rome to study. He became a *focolarino* two years later. Two of Eli's sisters would follow suit.

The consecrated *focolarini*, like the first Christians, put all their property in common. When the Folonari father died, in agreement with their mother, the children decided that the family wine business should go to the other brothers and that those who were in the Focolare would receive a different patrimony. Vincenzo inherited a farm and estate near Florence, at a place called Loppiano. In 1964 Vincenzo and others became the first inhabitants of what would become the first Focolare "little town" of Loppiano. In fact, as the summer gatherings held first at Tonadico, and then in all the countries and regions where the movement was present, were nicknamed a Mariapolis, so this "little town" and the others which would follow became known as a Permanent Mariapolis.

Loppiano has continued to grow and develop over the years and decades and is a fully functioning little town. It also became a place in which aspiring *focolarini* would spend a year of their formation before making their final consecration. Today it also houses the movement's university college, Sophia Institute.

Mariopolises

There are some twenty permanent Mariopolises around the world today. Once, when visiting with Don Foresi the town known as Aracoeli, in Brazil, in 1991, Chiara could not help but notice all the surrounding favelas there on the outskirts of Sao Paolo. Pope St John Paul II had recently issued his encyclical *Centesimus Annus*, on the hundredth anniversary of Pope Leo XIII's encyclical *Rerum Novarum*, considered the founding document of the Church's modern day Social Teaching.

At a talk to the assembled women and men *focolarini* there in Aracoeli one day, Chiara commented how different permanent Mariapolises of the movement had their own characteristics: Tagaytay with its study of and outreach to eastern religions, Ottmaring with relations between Catholics and other Christians. She recalled her original inspiration for the little towns, Einsiedeln:

> I felt that God wanted something similar from us, that God also wanted a little city from us, a real and true little city with houses, especially little houses, but also larger ones, with community centres, with factories, with businesses and industries.

She went on to say she had been reading the Pope's latest encyclical, *Centesimus Annus*. In that document, said Chiara, the Pope who had lived under the Communist yoke once again spoke against Communism and reaffirmed Christian social doctrine, which holds that private property is a right.

> He says that free enterprise is a right, that freedom to form associations (i.e. co-operatives, unions etc) is a right. He says that we must safeguard human rights under all aspects. However, he also speaks very much about solidarity, about the need to consider not only ourselves but others.
>
> So now you know how we've been thinking in recent days: Einsiedeln…the encyclical *Centesimus Annus*. At this point we began to consider our Ideal. We understood that our Ideal is a charism, but in our charism there is also a social aspect: it's a charism with a social background too. It's a charism which leads to sanctity; it's a charism which leads to ecumenical activities; it's a charism which leads to evangelisation; it's a charism which can help to resolve social problems.

She then went on to outline her vision of how a new way of economic life might take birth right there in their Mariapolis in Brazil and from there spread to all the other Mariapolises and to wherever the Focolare was present.

An Economy of Communion

What she explained was: as each permanent Mariapolis had its own enterprises, why not reach out and invite other businesses in the surrounding area to co-operate with them? What was new was that as a movement they would own and share capital, but the profits would be put in common. The profits would be used for good works. One third of the profits would go to helping those in need so that, like the early Christians, there should be no one in need among them. Another one third of the profits would be re-invested in the enterprise itself for its growth and development. The final third would be used to build, develop and support the little cities of the movement - because their purpose was to form "new" people who would be "pillars" of a new society where there would be a communion of goods.

Ever-practical, Chiara outlined how the residents of this little town of Aracoeli should start off. They should open a mini-industrial zone; not right there in the town, but further off on the estate; they should decide which local businesses to invite to co-operate with them and so on.

And she was quite clear: people from far and wide would come to study this new economic model. She was proved right. Economists have travelled from all over the world to study it. Students in different countries have written theses on it. In 1995 a Brazilian sociologist spoke about it to a conference at Lublin University in Poland, where Pope St John Paul II once lectured.

Honorary Doctorates

The following year Lublin University awarded Chiara an honorary doctorate in Social Sciences. It would be the first of some twenty such honorary doctorates she would be awarded in the final ten years of her life. Many were the towns and cities, universities, international organisations which wanted to confer honours on her. She once explained to her biographer that in deciding which to accept she was led by the guidance of her movement's Council and ultimately obeyed her immediate religious superiors in the relevant Vatican dicastery.

In 1998, leading up to the Great Jubilee of the year 2000, Pope St John Paul II decided to bring together all the new movements and communities in the Church. For three days a *World Congress of Ecclesial Movements* was held in Rome. Then, over two hundred thousand members of these movements gathered around this particularly Marian pope in St Peter's Square on the vigil of Pentecost.

Addressing the almost quarter of a million people in front of him, the Pope said, "It is as though what happened in Jerusalem two thousand years ago were being repeated this evening in this square, the heart of the Christian world."

He pointed out, "Today's event is truly unprecedented; for the first time the movements and the new ecclesial communities have all gathered together with the Pope."

And as he had previously explained to Chiara when he spoke of the Petrine and Marian profiles of the Church, so he repeated publicly now, "The institutional and charismatic aspects are co-essential to the Church's constitution. They contribute, albeit differently, to the life, renewal and sanctification of God's people."

Promise to the Pope

When it was the turn of Chiara, as leader of the largest of these new movements, to address the Pope, she stood at the microphone, looked directly at the Successor of St Peter and made a promise. As foundress and President of the Focolare, the Work of Mary, she said,

> We know that the Church, and you yourself, desire full communion, unity among the movements, and this has already begun. We want to assure you, Your Holiness, that because our specific charism is unity, we will make every effort to contribute, *with all our strength*, towards fully accomplishing it."

As after any contact with the Supreme Pontiff, Chiara returned to her home at the Focolare's administrative headquarters, in Rocca di Papa outside Rome, newly invigorated. She set up a new "Secretariat", a section within her movement, to work for and facilitate unity between the different movements. "From now on," she told her *focolarini*, "we must consider everything that is ours as belonging to *all* the movements in the Church."

Chiara greets Don Luigi Guissani, founder of Communione e Liberazione, during Pope St John Paul II's World Congress of Ecclesial Movements at Pentecost 1998.

In 2001 at Speyer in Germany, along with the Sant'Egidio Community and the Charismatic Renewal Movement, she was one of the organisers of a meeting of founders and leaders of over forty ecclesial movements and new communities. Pope St John Paul II sent a message of encouragement. As Chiara was acutely aware, what the Lord wanted, what the Vicar of Christ wanted and offered to Catholics, was also for the good of *all* humanity.

Later that same year, in Munich, Germany, a "Pact of Reciprocal Love" was drawn up and signed by some six hundred leaders of both Catholic and Protestant communities and movements. "From then on," remembered her faithful secretary Eli, "Chiara encouraged all of us in the Focolare to love the other movements as we loved our own. This was part of Jesus's commandment to love our neighbour as ourself."

Never one for sitting around and looking inwards, Chiara and her movement encouraged these newly-united leaders to reach out to the wider community, particularly at first in Europe, where Christian values were coming under increasing attack.

A Wider Community

Together for…

In 2004, when the European Community increased in size to twenty-five members, the various movements organized a day congress in Stuttgart, entitled *Together for Europe*. This was the fruit of some one hundred and fifty movements co-operating. The politicians attending included even the President of the European Commission, Romano Prodi. Addressing the thousands who gathered at that congress, Chiara quoted from Pope St John Paul II's 1998 Pentecost talk and she pointed out that as these new movements consisted primarily of lay people, "their actions have repercussions in the civic field, to which they offer concrete political, economic and social achievements." So, all this coming together had to be for a specific and good purpose.

Again in Stuttgart, in 2007, another *Together for Europe* day was held. It produced a type of manifesto. Known as the *Stuttgart Message*, it comprised a seven-fold Yes: Yes to life; Yes to the family; Yes to creation; Yes to a just economy; Yes to solidarity; Yes to peace; Yes to our responsibility towards the whole of society.

From being called together around the person of the Pope, the charisms present in the Church have gone on to grow more united, all the while safeguarding each one's own uniqueness. From taking the step of *being together*, under the leadership or common service of Chiara and her Focolare, they progressed to being *Together for…*

Since then a whole network has grown of more than a thousand "Towns for Europe" and the idea is being taken up on other continents too.

Ever Greater Unity

Chiara, now in her ninth decade, seemed to be invigorated with a new energy. Her collaborators and her movement had to run to keep up with her. A charism, she understood, was given for the good of the Church, therefore for the good of all. It could not, should not, limit itself to this or that aspect of life. Instead, as a gift from God, it must be welcomed into, and permeate all aspects of human society; in fact an inundation. She took the word from St John Chrysostom and it describes a flowing-into, like waves of the sea flowing onto and seeping into the seashore. The charism given by Almighty God to her, welcomed and lived by her and her millions of followers, should be carried forward, offered to, introduced to, all aspects of human endeavour.

She once wrote:

…Therefore what is his is mine, and nothing else. And his is universal suffering, and therefore mine. I will go through the world seeking it in every instant of my life. …In this way I will dry up the waters of tribulation in many hearts nearby, and through communion with my almighty Spouse, in many far away. I shall pass as a fire that consumes all that must fall and leaves standing only the truth.

So today, those who follow Chiara's "way", who live the Ideal of God-Love in Jesus Forsaken and the Desolate Mother, seek to bring the charism of unity into every area of their lives, not only personal but professional. On an institutional level, the worldwide movement "initiated" by a young primary school teacher from Trent organises get-togethers, symposia, congresses for people involved in specific fields, from the worlds of politics, law and education to those of sport, psychology, sociology; from architecture, medicine and media to art, economy and ecology.

It is as Chiara had written to Brother Jerome all those years ago, "I want you to know that Jesus Forsaken is everything. He is the guarantee of unity. All light on unity flows forth from that cry…" (that is, "My God, my God; Eli, Eli…")

Invigorated by the encounter with the Holy Father at Pentecost and her solemn promise to him, Chiara put all her strength and resources into the service of unity between movements, unity between people within the Church and those still outside the Church, people of all faiths and none. Her collaborators confessed privately, "We're struggling to keep up with her." And it was not only on a practical organisational level. For Chiara was calling them to ever-greater union with Jesus Forsaken, ever-greater mutual charity and self-giving.

Apart from preparing speeches for major events, receiving delegations from the zones of her movement around the world, keeping up with daily and weekly reports received from all the *focolares* and regions worldwide, receiving episcopal visitors, Chiara was also responding to literally thousands of letters every week.

A Serene Life

But she led a very ordered life. She herself described it to her biographer as "serene". Her office opened onto a chapel with the reserved Blessed Sacrament. She had her times of prayer during the day. Mealtimes were with her housemates, some of those "first companions". Because of recurrent spinal problems, she also obeyed her doctor and had a swim several times a week.

As they had done for the half a century of living in Rome and Rocca di Papa, in the afternoons Eli and Chiara would escape for a drive in the countryside. The work and cares of the movement would be left behind. They might listen to some music on a CD. Usually they would stop somewhere for a little walk as they prayed the Rosary together.

"I don't feel very well"

Coming back from such a drive one day, in late September 2004, as they arrived at the house, Chiara suddenly said, "I don't feel very well." At that moment, remembered Eli, "Chiara seemed to lose all energy, all strength". Her health did in fact fail dramatically. But this was no surprise to her friends and associates. As Eli put it, it was "the result of a long life lived with such intensity".

From that day on, Chiara undertook no further public engagements. She did, though, continue to follow developments in her movement. Eventually, without the strength to write, after hearing the reports from various zones and sections of the Work, she would dictate a phrase, sometimes only a word, to Eli, to send to the people concerned.

Her colleagues also installed a TV link-up between her house and the Movement's massive congress centre at Castel Gandolfo, so that Chiara could sometimes follow what was happening there on particular days. In fact, that congress centre had been built as an audience hall by Pope Pius XII. Pope St John Paul II, for his part, decided that he would not have all those thousands of pilgrims trekking out from Rome to visit him for an audience at Castel Gandolfo during the summer, but he instead would go to them. After all, a short helicopter ride could transport just him and his secretary to Rome in a matter of minutes.

As it was lying empty and unused, Pope St John Paul II put the former audience hall at the disposal of the Focolare, who converted and fitted it out into a superb multi-level congress centre. Pope St John Paul II himself used sometimes to take a walk through his gardens at Castel Gandolfo and through a gate in their adjoining "garden wall" he would visit the Focolare centre. Pope Benedict XVI visited every summer and offered Holy Mass in the congress centre's chapel for his visiting former pupils who held their annual reunions there.

So, linked up to this constantly busy congress centre, Chiara could watch proceedings. Sometimes, when she had strength, she would speak a word to the participants there, particularly if it was a youth gathering. "Even though you can't see me," she told them once, "Know that I'm always with you, always united to you."

One of the last visits that Chiara received at her home was a little delegation from England's Liverpool Hope University. Her burgeoning university Sophia Institute at Loppiano had formed reciprocal links with this and some other universities. Liverpool Hope conferred on Chiara her final honorary doctorate.

Steps prepared for us by God's love

In November 2006 Chiara suffered a bout of pneumonia for which she was hospitalised in the Gemelli polyclinic in Rome. During her stays in the Gemelli in her final years, Chiara would be given a room with a view towards the dome of St Peter's basilica.

Recovered from this episode, she returned home to Rocca di Papa but her respiratory function continued to deteriorate. She relied on oxygen and speaking became more and more difficult for her.

"Have we lived the Gospel?"

In the final year of her life, her housemates gave her a nicely-bound set of the four Gospels in a larger print. As she had done throughout her life, Chiara constantly read the Gospels. Continuing her lifelong habit, she would note thoughts, questions, clarifications in the margins in pencil.

In her final months she once shared with her housemates that she was reading and re-reading the Gospels "to see if there is anything in them that we have not lived, that we have not responded to or been faithful to." When they asked her what conclusion she had come to, she said, "Yes, I think we have responded to everything there. We have lived the Gospel message to the best of our ability."

As Chiara had experienced the "dark night of the soul", particularly in 1952, so in her last years and months she may have gone through other periods of darkness, particularly during 2005-2006. "Yet," said Eli, "I can testify that even during the period of interior trials, Chiara never stopped loving. Loving everyone. Right to the end."

Chiara had once written about death:

> We must see illnesses that come upon us as steps prepared for us by God's love…for the complete *consummatum est* ["it is finished"] which awaits us all. Lord, let us run without reluctance towards the goal we must soon reach. Help us to give you everything of ourselves before death - like a thief - robs us of it. Help us to offer you the most beautiful thing we have, like the Father gave his only Son, like Mary her Son, like every saint their work. Thus, nothing will change for us when you call us, and death will be a splendid and almost unremarkable passage in unity with you who desired to take on our flesh to precede us.

During her final illness she once remarked to Eli, "I no longer feel like Chiara. It seems like I'm only Silvia". It appeared she was stripped of all attachment, even to her life's work.

On 3rd February 2008 Chiara had a routine appointment for a check-up with her consultants at the Gemelli. She seemed to be doing well; but when she reached the

The Year of the Family (1994). Chiara addresses tens of thousands of her movement's young people, the 'Gen' (new generations) at a sports stadium in Rome.

hospital she broke out in a fever. They decided to keep her in. Her condition deteriorated quickly. It was another bout of pneumonia. She was rushed into intensive care.

Day followed day and the doctors would not discharge her. As her physical strength dissipated and she understood that death was drawing near, Chiara, so it seemed to Eli, became even more Christ-like. At one point one of her lungs had become completely blocked and the medical staff had to carry out an extremely painful procedure to clear it. Chiara said simply, "I offer this for the Work."

Even while she was still at home, remembered Eli, after Holy Communion every day Chiara would pray for the Work of Mary and then add, "for all the sinners in the world", or sometimes, "Let us entrust to Our Lady all those who will die today, those who died yesterday and those who will die in the future." At other times she would pray "for all the dying, that Jesus may save them," and "not only for our own sick, but for all the sick and dying in the world."

Telegram from the Pope

On 3rd March 2008 a telegram arrived at the hospital:

Dear Signorina Chiara, I am aware of the trial which you are undergoing and wish to assure you, in this difficult time, of my prayer that the Lord may grant you physical relief, spiritual comfort and, demonstrating

Chiara with Pope St John Paul II. Immediately after his election he invited Chiara and Eli to his private Mass in the Apostolic Palace, before his inauguration even. As Pope Benedict XVI later wrote, "The sure guiding light for her was the thinking of the Pope."

to you his benevolence, may grant you to experience the redemptive value of suffering lived in profound communion with him. With this prayer, from my heart I grant you a special Apostolic Blessing, as a pledge of abundant outpourings of heavenly favours.

Benedict XVI

Reading the Pope's reference to the "redemptive value of suffering", Eli recalled how Chiara had often remarked, "I offer my pain for all the sinners of the world".

On the 6th March Eli received a telephone call. The Ecumenical Patriarch of Constantinople was on a visit to Rome and wished to call on Chiara. His All-Holiness Bartholomew arrived at the Gemelli later that same day. At Chiara's bedside, he said, "Chiara, I really wanted to come and see you, to tell you that I am praying for you." He thanked her for all that she had done for the entire Church of Christ, and then he presented her with a gold cross. Then he leaned over her bed and embraced her, gave her a great big hug.

"The Madonna!"

On 11th March Eli was sitting on one side of the bed, and another of Chiara's housemates, a Swiss *focolarina* named Anna Paula Meyer, on the other. They both saw that Chiara was trying to tell them something but they couldn't understand because of the oxygen mask. Then, suddenly, she said strongly and very clearly, "Our Lady!" ("La Madonna!") She was looking at a fixed point in front of her, right at the end of her bed. They felt an atmosphere of complete and utter serenity and it appeared that Chiara was in conversation with someone. They both remember that this lasted for several minutes.

"From that moment," said Eli, "she entered into a new serenity. It seemed that she no longer suffered any physical pain." In the days before this event, Chiara had often said to her companions, "Why don't we go home now?" Eli remembered that this brought a lump to her throat as she recalled how Chiara had once written that often when elderly people ask to go home, they are really yearning for their heavenly home.

Eli remembered:

I had to tell her. Because Chiara always went to the *focolarini* who were dying [amongst the hundreds of *focolarini* who lived around the "headquarters" at Rocca di Papa]. She was always the one who went to them to let them know that the moment of "departure" was approaching. It was a work of mercy that she took seriously.

So I spoke to her, saying, "Chiara, the moment of your meeting with Jesus is arriving. From everything that you have shown us of Paradise, it will be a marvellous meeting." And somehow it came to me to speak of heaven, I don't know where I got all these words! And she started to smile, to smile, to smile! It was a truly beautiful moment.

"Bring me home"

From suggesting and asking, Chiara then began to become more insistent. "Bring me home. Bring me home." At first her medical professor consultant was hesitant. Then he realised that there was nothing more to be done for her medically, so, on the evening of 12th March 2008, arrangements were put in place. An ambulance transported her speedily that same night from Rome, arriving at her home in Rocca di Papa at midnight.

When Chiara opened her eyes the next morning, Anna Paula said to her, "See, Chiara? You're at home, in your own room, with your two loves there in front of you." Chiara looked and saw the two paintings on the wall at the foot of her bed: Jesus Forsaken and Mary Desolate Mother. Then she looked to her right, saw through the window her little garden and nodded and smiled. She was happy to be home.

Then Don Foresi, the first *focolarino* to be ordained a priest, and whom she called a "co-founder", arrived and offered Holy Mass. A short while later Chiara managed to receive a fragment of Holy Communion, the Eucharistic Jesus. Then, one by one, her first companions arrived and each had a moment with her. She was alert and knew each of them. When one of them (Vale) said, "We'll see each other again in heaven!" Chiara responded "You are right! I'll be waiting for you!"

From the moment that the ambulance had pulled up the night before, word got out that Chiara was home. People began to gather outside her house and in the grounds of the Centre of the Movement. With daylight and throughout the day the crowds began to swell. All these people had been inspired by Chiara to give their lives to God, to live her Ideal of Jesus Forsaken, Unity, Jesus in the midst. They wanted to remain near to her, to let her know they were with her, accompanying her on her final journey. They gently sang hymns and Focolare songs.

After her first companions had all greeted her, Anna Paula and Chiara's doctor and housemate Doni spoke to one another. Seeing the massed crowds outside they said, "Chiara belongs to everyone. She often told us, 'I am made for everyone'." And so the decision was taken to throw open the doors of Chiara's house. Hour after hour for the rest of the day, the line of those coming to greet Chiara seemed endless. To many she was a spiritual mother, to others a sister, to all an inspiration.

She loved them to the end

This final meeting with so many hundreds of her "followers" in her final hours made Eli think of the phrase in St John's Gospel, "And having loved them, he loved them to the end." Hour after hour they processed through her room. Many kissed her hand. Some said simply "Thank you", others, "We will never forget you Chiara". Some asked pardon from her. Others vowed to continue living as she had taught them. Chiara acknowledged each person, sometimes mouthing "Yes", sometimes squeezing a hand, other times a nod of the head.

By about 9.30 that evening her housemates could see that Chiara was tiring and they decided to close the doors on the crowds who were still gathering and queueing outside. Shortly after that one of the first male *focolarini*, a priest, arrived home from a trip. He arrived at Chiara's house around 10 p.m. and could see that she was evidently not much longer for this world.

"Chiara," he said, "You're returning to the heart of the Father, to remain there forever." Chiara seemed to recover her voice. Clearly and strongly she declared, "Yes." It was the last word she ever pronounced. The young girl who had spoken her "yes", her *fiat*, in that early-morning ceremony so many years before, now uttered her final, heartfelt "yes" to God.

A serene calmness reigned throughout Chiara's house. The crowds outside had quietly dispersed. A couple of hours later when Chiara's doctor (Doni) observed that her blood pressure had dropped dramatically, she summoned the other members of the household. They gathered around the bed in prayer, reciting the Rosary. When they were praying the *Salve Regina*, at about two o'clock in the morning, that 14th March, Chiara breathed her last.

A world of Catholic reading at your fingertips...

Catholic Faith, Life & Truth for all

www.CTSbooks.org

twitter: @CTSpublishers

facebook.com/CTSpublishers

Catholic Truth Society, Publishers to the Holy See.